LIVIN' LA VIDA DORKA

The Complete Dork Tower Comic Strip Collection, Vol. I

by John Kovalic

WITHDRAWN

DORK STORM PRESS

OTHER BOOKS BY JOHN KOVALIC:

Dork Covenant: The Collected Dork Tower Comic Books, I

Dork Shadows: The Collected Dork Tower Comic Books, II

Heart of Dorkness: The Collected Dork Tower Comic Books, III*

Wild Life: The Cardinal Collection

The Wild Life Journals

The Wild Life Files

* Available Spring 2002

Dork Storm Press
PO Box 45063,
Madison, WI 53744
http://www.dorkstorm.com

Marketing, sales and advertising inquiries:
sales@dorkstorm.com
Phone: (608) 255-1348 • Fax (608) 442-1528

Editorial and other inquiries:
john@kovalic.com.

Cover design, interior design and layout: Aaron Williams

PRINTED IN CANADA • FIRST PRINTING, January 2002 • ISBN 1-930964-42-0

To Aaron Williams, a great
colleague, and a great friend.

INTRODUCTION
by Scott Kurtz

John Kovalic has been my guide in the world of self-publishing.

It started with a frantic cell phone call. It was October of 2000 and I was driving nonstop from Dallas to St. Louis to meet him and his friend, Dork Storm Press' other cofounder and cartoonist Aaron Williams. Rather than make the trips in two days, I decided to push it and go all the way in one.

It got dark, I got lost, and John got a succession of phone calls at 10 PM.

"I think I know where you are, Scott," he said. "Take your next right and you'll end back up on the highway." I apologized for calling so late, so often, and so upset. "No problem at all," he assured me.

The next day, John, Aaron and I plotted out the following year on a legal pad. They had been publishing their comic books for a couple of years, and this was the first time I had ever met them. We were deciding when the first issue of my comic, PvP, would be released, and how we would handle the costs of conventions and business.

I remember that day very fondly because it was the day Dork Storm Press adopted me into their family. John and Aaron had paved the way for my career in publishing by impressing retailers, readers and other creators with their talent and wit those previous years as the Dork Storm books became something of a mini phenomenon. It was the name they made for themselves that got me into stores around the world.

On my end, I was to be John and Aaron's guide into the world of online publishing. My comic strip started online and had built a substantial audience there. This is what I was bringing to the table. And so I worked my magic, phoned some of my contacts and got Gamespy.com to publish Dork Tower on their very popular website. Heck, that's the reason you're holding this book now. Right?

Wrong.

Not only did Gamespy pick up Dork Tower without my help, but John also put in a good word to them for me. He phoned some of his contacts and got Gamespy.com to publish PvP on their very popular website.

That job paid my rent and fed my family for a good while.

This collection of Dork Tower comics (from Gamespy, Interactive Week and elsewhere) proves that John never really needed my help as far as online comic strips go. As proud as I am of my accomplishments and as much as John insists that I'm "the master of the online comic strip", the truth is that I owe a lot of my success this last year to him.

John likes to say that I force him to be a better cartoonist.

The feeling is mutual.

Scott R. Kurtz
PvPonline.com
Dallas, Texas
January 3, 2002

HOME

ARCHIVES

STORE

RAMBLINGS

WHO'S WHO

DOWNLOADS

GALLERY

FAQs

GOT DORKS

MEET JOHN

FEEDBACK

LINKS

EMAIL LISTS

CLUB DORK

BOARDS

About this volume

Livin' La Vida Dorka is a collection of Dork Tower comic strips, the vast majority of which have never been gathered in print before. The sections (Pyramid; DorkTower.com/ GameSpy.com; Interactive Week; Scrye) are arranged in chronological order of the strips being picked up by the various publications.

About a half dozen comic strips contained here HAVE appeared in the comic books. For the sake of completeness of their various sections, I left them in.

Pyramid (pages 9-25)

Most of the comic strips that have been published in Pyramid magazine have already been collected in the regular Dork Tower comic books and comic book compilations. However, a few haven't. These ran in "The Dork Tower Swimsuit Special." Few people saw or preordered "The Dork Tower Swimsuit Special," since I chose to title it "The Dork Tower Swimsuit Special" and not "A Whole Bunch of Gaming-Related Comic Strips That You'll Probably Really, Really Like If You Enjoy The Regular Comic Book."

You live and learn. In the meantime, here are the Pyramid comic strips from the Swimsuit Special at last.

Dorktower.com/GameSpy.com (pages 27-85)

Dork Tower is hosted online by Gamespy.com, and most of these strips deal with computer and console gaming. New material appears there three times a week, God willing and the creek don't rise. The first two strips about Matt's brother Simon actually appeared in Pyramid. I moved them to this section, since they fit in with the overall flow better here.

Interactive Week (pages 87-141)

Interactive Week was a hugely successful, fabulously wealthy Ziff-Davis magazine with a circulation of nearly half a million. Dork Tower began running there in December, 2000. Within a year the publication folded.

I like to believe those two events are in no way connected. The causality of it all haunts me, however.

These 'toons probably represent my most mainstream work to date, save for my editorial cartoons. Certainly, these are some of my favorite strips, and I was privileged to work with some great editors there who (I believe) somehow managed to bring out the best in me. The fan mail poured in from IW readers, and this gig was a definite highlight of my professional career.

The I-Manager series that ends this section was an Interactive Week cover story commissioned by Editor in Chief Rob Fixmer. I'd like to thank him for MANY sleepless nights I spent worrying that I'd flub the assignment and look like a fool in front of 400,000 readers. On the plus side, the story was received with wild enthusiasm. Proving what? I fear to think...

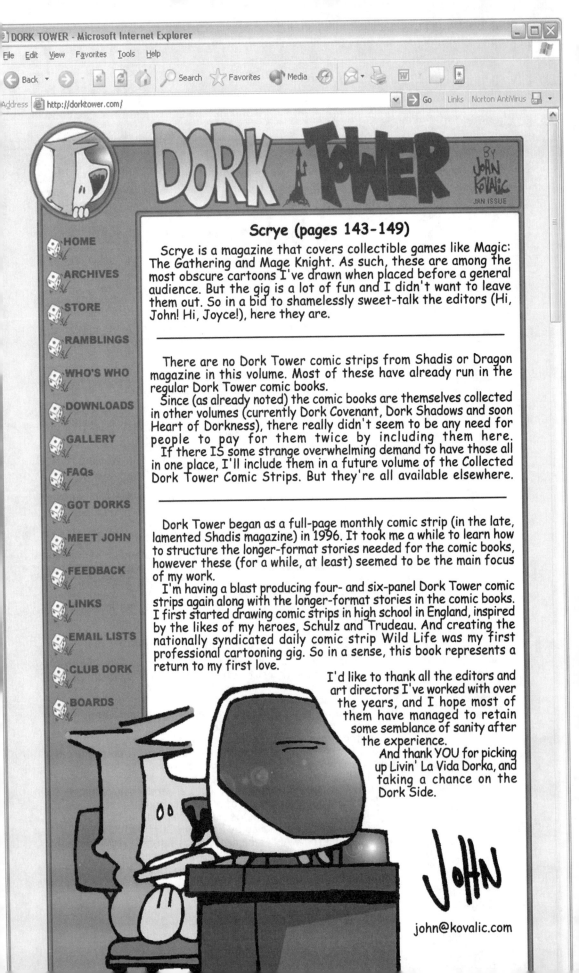

DORK TOWER BY JOHN KOVALIC

JAN ISSUE

HOME
ARCHIVES
STORE
RAMBLINGS
WHO'S WHO
DOWNLOADS
GALLERY
FAQs
GOT DORKS
MEET JOHN
FEEDBACK
LINKS
EMAIL LISTS
CLUB DORK
BOARDS

Scrye (pages 143-149)

Scrye is a magazine that covers collectible games like Magic: The Gathering and Mage Knight. As such, these are among the most obscure cartoons I've drawn when placed before a general audience. But the gig is a lot of fun and I didn't want to leave them out. So in a bid to shamelessly sweet-talk the editors (Hi, John! Hi, Joyce!), here they are.

There are no Dork Tower comic strips from Shadis or Dragon magazine in this volume. Most of these have already run in the regular Dork Tower comic books.

Since (as already noted) the comic books are themselves collected in other volumes (currently Dork Covenant, Dork Shadows and soon Heart of Dorkness), there really didn't seem to be any need for people to pay for them twice by including them here.

If there IS some strange overwhelming demand to have those all in one place, I'll include them in a future volume of the Collected Dork Tower Comic Strips. But they're all available elsewhere.

Dork Tower began as a full-page monthly comic strip (in the late, lamented Shadis magazine) in 1996. It took me a while to learn how to structure the longer-format stories needed for the comic books, however these (for a while, at least) seemed to be the main focus of my work.

I'm having a blast producing four- and six-panel Dork Tower comic strips again along with the longer-format stories in the comic books. I first started drawing comic strips in high school in England, inspired by the likes of my heroes, Schulz and Trudeau. And creating the nationally syndicated daily comic strip Wild Life was my first professional cartooning gig. So in a sense, this book represents a return to my first love.

I'd like to thank all the editors and art directors I've worked with over the years, and I hope most of them have managed to retain some semblance of sanity after the experience.

And thank YOU for picking up Livin' La Vida Dorka, and taking a chance on the Dork Side.

John

john@kovalic.com

"...only in consumption, endless consumption, could they escape the amorphous threat of the invisible fnords."

-Robert Shea, Robert Anton-Wilson:
"The Illuminati."

14

"What manner of men are these against whom you have sent us to fight - men who compete in their games not for money, but for honor?"

-Herodotus (484 - 425 BC)

51

65

66

69

70

Time is an illusion. Lunchtime doubly so.

The Hitch-Hiker's Guide to the Galaxy

71

81

Interactive Ⓘ Week

"Computer, if you don't open that exit hatch pretty damn pronto, I shall go straight to your major data banks with a very large ax and give you a reprogramming you will never forget!"

- *Zaphod Beeblebrox,*
  "Hitchhiker's Guide to the Galaxy"
  by Douglas Adams

DORK TOWER BY JOHN KOVALIC

SO WHAT ARE PEOPLE WISHING FOR THIS YEAR?

MAINLY AN END TO SPAM.

SPAM?

SPAM AND POP-UP MENUS, AND PEOPLE WHO FORWARD INANE JOKES TWELVE OTHER PEOPLE HAVE ALREADY FORWARDED YOU.

NORTH POLE

CLAUS

THAT AND CORPORATE WEB SITES THAT TAKE EONS TO LOAD, ARE MONTHS OUT OF DATE, CONTAIN NO ACTUAL USEFUL INFORMATION AND ARE WILLING TO SELL YOUR E-MAIL ADDRESS TO THE HIGHEST BIDDER.

LOTS OF WISHES FOR OPERATING SYSTEMS THAT DON'T CRASH AND RELEASE DATES THAT ARE MET, AND FOR AN END TO VAPOWARE, INTERNET HOAXES AND DEAD LINKS. WISHES FOR SOFTWARE THAT'S BUG-FREE AND COMEDIANS WHO REFRAIN FROM USING THE PHRASE "DOT COM" AS PART OF A PUNCHLINE OR PUN.

OH, YES: AND TRADITIONAL MEDIA OUTLETS DOING SOMETHING OTHER THAN PREDICTING THE DEATH OF THE NEW ECONOMY, SHOWING A BASIC UNDER-STANDING OF THE ELECTRONIC AGE THEY'RE REPORTING ON, OR EVEN JUST DEMONSTRATING THAT THEY HAVE A CLUE...

EXPECTATIONS WERE SO MUCH MORE REALISTIC WHEN ALL FOLKS ASKED FOR WAS PEACE ON EARTH...

NOW, THE NEXT 14 PAGES ALL SEEM TO DEAL WITH "MICROSOFT WORD"...

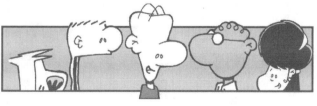

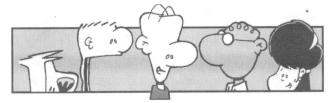

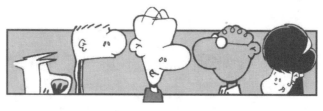

DORK TOWER BY JOHN KOVALIC

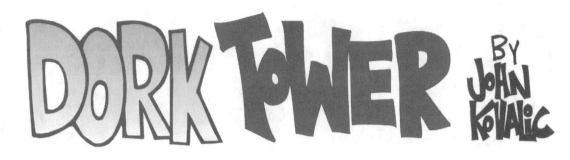

DORK TOWER
BY JOHN KOVALIC

WE RECEIVED A PIECE OF SPAM THE OTHER WEEK...

To: john@kovalic.com
Subject: System Administrator Appreciation Day

Friday, July 27th, 2001, is System Administrator Appreciation Day. On this special international day, give your System Administrator something that shows that you truly appreciate their hard work and dedication. Let's face it, System Administrators get no respect 364 days a year. We are asking for a nice token gift and some public acknowledgement. Maybe cake and ice cream. It's the least you could do. Consider all ~~the~~ (and pizza, too) the daunting tasks and ~~~~

NOW, SOME OF OUR BEST FRIENDS ARE SYSTEM ADMINISTRATORS (PARTICULARLY WHEN WE NEED THEIR HELP WITH SMALL PROBLEMS).

SWEET MOTHER OF MERCY, THE ENTIRE NETWORK'S MELTING!~

SO ENJOY A TRADITIONAL SYSTEM ADMINISTRATOR APPRECIATION DAY, EVERYONE!

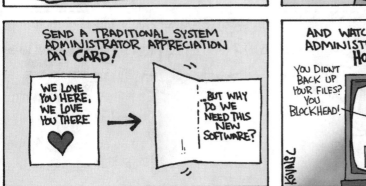

HAVE A TRADITIONAL SYSTEM ADMINISTRATOR APPRECIATION DAY MEAL!

PIZZA HAUS
MOUNTAIN DEW

GIVE A TRADITIONAL SYSTEM ADMINISTRATOR APPRECIATION DAY GREETING!

SYSTEM'S DOWN!

SYSTEM'S DOWN TO YOU, TOO!

SEND A TRADITIONAL SYSTEM ADMINISTRATOR APPRECIATION DAY CARD!

WE LOVE YOU HERE, WE LOVE YOU THERE ♥

...BUT WHY DO WE NEED THIS NEW SOFTWARE?

AND WATCH A TRADITIONAL SYSTEM ADMINISTRATOR APPRECIATION DAY HOLIDAY SPECIAL!

YOU DIDN'T BACK UP YOUR FILES? YOU BLOCKHEAD!

Hallmark presents: It's System Administrator Appreciation Day, Charlie Brown!

KOVALIC

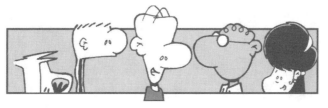

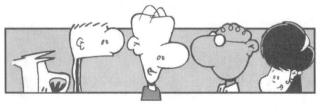

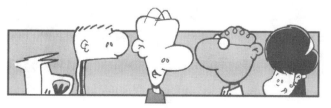

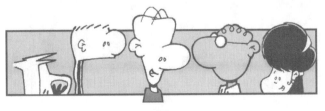

A FIELD GUIDE To i-managers

AT THE TURN OF THE 21st CENTURY, A NEW **BREED** OF PEOPLE CAME INTO THEIR OWN. A PEOPLE WHO, THROUGH THE APPLICATION OF TECHNOLOGY, HELD THE POWER TO SHAPE **THE COUNTRY**, ITS **ECONOMY** ... NAY... **THE VERY WORLD** FOR GENERATIONS TO COME.

NO... NOT FLORIDA VOTERS AND BUTTERFLY BALLOTS. **I-MANAGERS** AND THE **INTERNET!**

LET'S TAKE A LOOK AT THIS MYSTERIOUS BREED. JOIN US, WON'T YOU, FOR

A FIELD GUIDE to I-managers
BY JOHN KOVALIC

WE'RE HERE OBSERVING AN I-MANAGER IN ITS **NATURAL HABITAT.**

SHHHH. THAT SOUND YOU HEAR IS ITS **DISTRESS CRY...**

MORE BANDWIDTH! MORE BANDWIDTH! MORE BANDWIDTH! MORE BANDWIDTH! MORE BANDWIDTH!

JUST WHO **ARE** THESE I-MANAGERS, AND **WHERE** DO THEY COME FROM?

LONG BEFORE THERE WAS AN **INTERNET**, THERE WERE **PIONEERS** DEDICATED TO **FORGING** NEW **FRONTIERS** OF **TECHNOLOGY, COMMERCE** AND **COMMUNICATION.** TODAY, WE RECOGNIZE THEM AS THE **COMMON ANCESTORS** OF MODERN I-MANAGERS.

SCRYE

THE GUIDE TO COLLECTIBLE CARD GAMES

"... For me there are more hours of amusement in a single deck of cards than in all the world's movies combined. And I love the movies."
-Richard Garfield

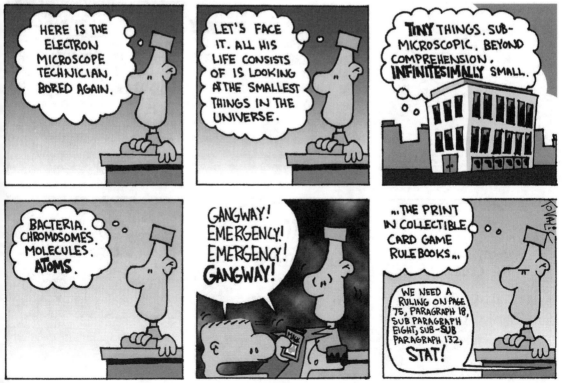

About the Author

John Kovalic was born in Manchester, England, in 1962. Dork Tower began in SHADIS magazine in 1996, and the multi-Origins award-nominated Dork Tower comic book was launched in June 1998. The first issue sold out in eight weeks to fantastic reviews and tremendous industry buzz. John's award-winning editorial cartoons appear everywhere from his hometown WISCONSIN STATE JOURNAL and CAPITAL TIMES (Madison, WI) to the NEW YORK TIMES and the WASHINGTON POST. His other creations include SnapDragons and Newbies (with Liz Rathke), Wild Life, Beached, the Unspeakable Oaf and many others.

One of the first cartoonists to put their work on the internet, his self-produced World Wide Web site, kovalic.com, has received numerous national and international kudos. If you ask him nicely, he'll tell you how he helped create GAMES Magazine's 1999 Party Game of the Year, the international best-selling, award-winning "Apples to Apples." He may even tell you how he once ended up in the pages of the National Enquirer.

His degree was in Economics with a minor in Astrophysics. In his spare time, John searches for spare time.

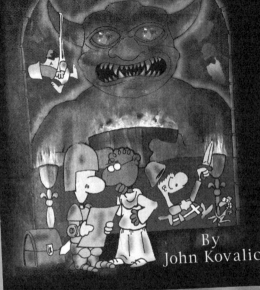